# SAME-SEX
## PARTNERSHIPS?

# SAME-SEX PARTNERSHIPS?

## A Christian Perspective

John Stott

Fleming H. Revell
A Division of Baker Book House
Grand Rapids, Michigan 49516

Published by Fleming H. Revell
a division of Baker Book House Company
P.O. Box 6287, Grand Rapids, MI 49516-6287

This paperback is the edited and updated chapter 16 of *Decisive Issues Facing Christians Today*, whose third edition will appear toward the end of 1999.

Printed in the United States of America

### Library of Congress Cataloging-in-Publication Data

Stott, John R. W.
    Same-sex partnerships?: a Christian perspective / John Stott.
       p.       cm.
    Includes bibliographical references.
    ISBN 0-8007-5674-6 (pbk.)
      1. Homosexuality—Religious aspects—Christianity—Controversial literature. 2. Gay couples. I. Title.
BR115.H6S765     1998
261.8'35766—dc21                         98-3789

All the royalties from this book have been irrevocably assigned to the Evangelical Literature Trust (U.K.), which distributes evangelical books to pastors, theological teachers and students, and seminary libraries in the developing world. Further information may be obtained from, and tax-deductible donations sent to, the evangelical literature program of John Stott Ministries, 871 Pinegrove Court, Wheaton, IL 60187.

# CONTENTS

# PREFACE

No ethical challenge facing the churches today is more radical than the homosexual or "gay" debate. It tends to be polarized between "homophobia" and "homophilia," that is, between those who feel an emotional revulsion towards homosexual people and those who regard committed same-sex relationships as morally equivalent to marriage.

Are we limited to this alternative? Or is it possible to disentangle our emotions from our convictions? Is there a Christian way to combine biblical thinking about God's intention for human sexuality with an equally biblical attitude of understanding, respect, and support for persons with a homosexual disposition?

This small paperback claims to be no more than a Christian contribution to the contemporary debate. I begin by revisiting the four main clusters of biblical material which express a negative stance towards homosexual practices, but I continue with the positive teaching in Genesis 1 and 2 about sexuality and marriage, which Jesus our Lord himself endorsed. I then listen carefully to the five main arguments which are advanced in favor of same-sex partnerships, and I seek to respond to them sensitively. Finally, after an excursus on the global AIDS epidemic, I conclude with the Christian call to faith, hope, and love as it relates to homosexual people.

This book is the revised and updated chapter 16 of *Decisive Issues Facing Christians Today,* which was first published in 1984 and a second edition of which appeared in 1990. The third edition, which takes account of developing debates during the 1990s, is due to be published towards the end of 1999. The publication of *Same-Sex Partnerships?* anticipates it.

*John Stott*

# 1

# THE CONTEXT

Because of the explosive nature of the topic, let me begin by describing the proper context for our thinking about same-sex partnerships and by affirming a number of truths about my readers and myself which I am taking for granted as I write.

## Four Affirmations

First, *we are all human beings*. That is to say, there is no such phenomenon as "a homosexual." There are only people, human persons, made in the image and likeness of God, yet fallen, with all the glory and the tragedy which that paradox implies, including sexual potential and sexual problems. However strongly we may disapprove of homosexual practices, we have no liberty to dehumanize those who engage in them.

Secondly, *we are all sexual beings.* Our sexuality, according to both Scripture and experience, is basic to our humanness. Angels may be sexless; we humans are not. When God made humankind, he made us male and female. So to talk about sex is to touch a point close to the center of our personality. A vital part of our identity is being discussed and perhaps either endorsed or threatened. So the subject demands an unusual degree of sensitivity.

Moreover, not only are we all sexual beings, but we all have a particular sexual inclination. American zoologist Alfred C. Kinsey's famous investigation into human sexuality led him to place every human being somewhere on a spectrum from zero (an exclusively heterosexual bias, attracted only to the opposite sex) to six (an exclusively homosexual bias, attracted only to the same sex, whether homosexual males or "lesbians," as homosexual females are usually called). In between these poles he plotted varying degrees of bisexuality, referring to people whose sexual inclination is dual or indeterminate or fluctuating.

Since the publication in 1948 of Kinsey's report on male sexual behavior,[1] he has been widely quoted as having found that 10 percent of American men (at least, of white American males) are exclusively homosexual throughout their lives. This is a serious misquotation, however. Ten percent was his figure for men who are predominantly homosexual for up to three years between the ages of sixteen and sixty-five. His figure for lifelong and exclusive homosexual men was 4 percent, and even this has been challenged on the ground that his sampling was not representative. More recent studies have found the incidence of homosexual practice to be lower still. According to four surveys conducted by the U.S. National Opinion Research Center between 1970 and 1990, the number of men who had had a homosexual encounter ever was 6 percent, and during the previous year 1.8 percent, while the percentage of the population which had adopted a consistently homosexual lifestyle was between 0.6 percent and 0.7 percent. A 1990–91 British survey found similarly that 1.1 percent had had a homosexual partner during the previous year. These studies suggest that in the western world less than 2 percent of the male population, and less than 1 percent of the female, are exclusively homosexual in inclination and practice.

Thirdly, *we are all sinners*. We are frail and vulnerable. We are pilgrims on our way to God. We are very far from having arrived. We are engaged in an unremitting conflict with the world, the flesh, and the devil. Not yet have we conquered. Perfection awaits the parousia. In addition and in particular, we are all sexual sinners. The doctrine of total depravity asserts that every part of our human being has been tainted and twisted by sin, and that this includes our sexuality. Dr. Merville Vincent, of the Department of Psychiatry at Harvard Medical School, is surely correct when he writes: "In God's view I suspect we are all sexual deviants. I doubt if there is anyone who has not had a lustful thought that deviated from God's perfect ideal of sexuality."[2] Nobody (with the sole exception of Jesus of Nazareth) has been sexually sinless. There is no question, therefore, of coming to this study with a horrid "holier than thou" attitude of moral superiority. Because all of us are sinners, we all stand under the judgment of God, and we are all in urgent need of the grace of God. Besides, sexual sins are not the only sins, nor even necessarily the most sinful; pride and hypocrisy are surely worse.

Fourthly, in addition to being human, sexual, and sinful creatures, I take it that *we are all Christians*. At least, the readers I have in mind are not people who reject the lordship of Jesus Christ but rather those who earnestly desire to submit to it, believe that he exercises it through Scripture, want to understand what light Scripture throws on this topic, and have a predisposition to seek God's grace to follow his will when it is known. Without this kind of commitment, it would be more difficult for us to find common ground. To be sure,

12

God's standards are the same for everybody, but non-Christian people are less ready to accept them.

## Three Necessary Distinctions

Having delineated the context for our discussion, I am ready to ask the question, Are homosexual partnerships a Christian option? I phrase my question advisedly. It introduces us to three necessary distinctions.

First, at least in Britain since the Wolfenden Report of 1957 and the resultant Sexual Offenses Act of 1967, we have learned to distinguish between sins and crimes. Adultery has always (according to God's law) been a sin, but in most countries it is not an offense punishable by the state. Rape, by contrast, is both a sin and a crime. What the Sexual Offenses Act of 1967 did was to declare that a homosexual act performed between consenting adults over twenty-one in private should no longer be a criminal offense. "The Act did not in fact 'legalize' such behavior," wrote Professor Sir Norman Anderson, "for it is still regarded by the law as immoral, and is devoid of any legal recognition; all the Act did was to remove the criminal sanction from such acts when performed in private between two consenting adults."[3]

Secondly, we have grown accustomed to distinguish between a homosexual inclination or "inversion" (for which people may not be responsible) and homosexual physical practices (for which they are). The importance of this distinction goes beyond the attribution of responsibility to the attribution of guilt. We may not blame people for what they are, though we may for what they do. And in every discussion about homosexuality we must be rigorous in differentiating between this "being" and "doing," that is, between a person's identity and activity, sexual preference and sexual practice, constitution and conduct.

But now we have to come to terms with a third distinction, namely between homosexual practices which are casual (and probably anonymous) acts of self-gratification and those which (it is claimed) are just as expressive of authentic human love as is heterosexual intercourse in marriage. No responsible homosexual person (whether Christian or not) is advocating promiscuous "one night stands," let alone violence or the corruption of young people and children. What some are arguing, however, especially in the Lesbian and Gay Christian Movement in Britain, is that a heterosexual marriage and a homosexual partnership are "two equally valid alternatives,"[4] being equally tender, mature, and faithful. In May 1989 Denmark became the first country to legalize homosexual marriages. The previous year Bishop

John S. Spong of Newark, New Jersey, urged the Episcopal Church "to bless and affirm the love that binds two persons of the same gender into a life-giving relationship of mutual commitment."[5]

The question before us, then, does not relate to homosexual practices of a casual nature but asks whether homosexual partnerships—lifelong and loving—are a Christian option. Our concern is to subject prevailing attitudes (which range from total revulsion to equally uncritical endorsement) to biblical scrutiny. Is our sexual "preference" purely a matter of personal taste? Or has God revealed his will regarding a norm? In particular, can the Bible be shown to sanction homosexual partnerships, or at least not to condemn them? What, in fact, does the Bible condemn?

# 2
# THE BIBLICAL PROHIBITIONS

The late Derrick Sherwin Bailey was the first Christian theologian to reevaluate the traditional understanding of the biblical prohibitions. His famous book, of which all subsequent writers on this topic have had to take careful account, namely *Homosexuality and the Western Christian Tradition,* was published in 1955. Although many have not been persuaded by his attempted reconstruction, in particular his reinterpretation of the sin of Sodom, there are other writers, less cautious in scholarly standards than he, who regard his argument as merely preliminary and build on his foundations a much more permissive position. It is essential to consider this debate.

## Biblical References to Homosexual Behavior

There are four main biblical passages which refer (or appear to refer) to the homosexual question negatively:

1. the story of Sodom (Gen. 19:1–13), with which it is natural to associate the very similar story of Gibeah (Judg. 19);
2. the Levitical texts (Lev. 18:22 and 20:13) which explicitly prohibit "lying with a man as one lies with a woman";
3. the apostle Paul's portrayal of decadent pagan society in his day (Rom. 1:18–32); and
4. two Pauline lists of sinners, each of which includes a reference to homosexual practices of some kind (1 Cor. 6:9–10 and 1 Tim. 1:8–11).

### The Stories of Sodom and Gibeah

The Genesis narrative makes it clear that "the men of Sodom were wicked and were sinning greatly against the LORD" (Gen. 13:13), and that "the outcry against Sodom and Gomorrah" was "so great and their sin so grievous" that God determined to investigate it (18:20–21). In the end God "overthrew those cities and the entire plain, including all those living in the cities" (19:25) by an act of judgment which was entirely consistent with the justice of "the Judge of all the earth" (18:25). There is no controversy about this background to the biblical story. The question is, What was the sin of the people of Sodom (and Gomorrah) which merited their obliteration?

The traditional Christian view has been that they were guilty of homosexual practices, which they attempted (unsuccessfully) to inflict on the two angels whom Lot was entertaining in his home. Hence the word "sodomy." But Bailey challenges this interpretation on two main grounds. First, it is a gratuitous assumption (he argues) that the demand of the men of Sodom "Bring them out to us, so that we may *know* them" meant "so that we can have sex with them" (NIV). For the Hebrew word for know *(yāda')* occurs 943 times in the Old Testament, of which only ten occurrences refer to physical intercourse, and even then only to heterosexual intercourse. It would therefore be better to translate the phrase "so that we may get acquainted with them." We can then understand the men's violence as due to their anger that Lot had exceeded his rights as a resident alien, for he had welcomed two strangers into his home "whose intentions might be hostile and whose credentials—had not been examined."[6] In this case the sin of Sodom was to invade the privacy of Lot's home and flout the ancient rules of hospitality. Lot begged them to desist, because, he said, the two men "have come under the protection of my roof" (19:8).

Bailey's second argument is that the rest of the Old Testament nowhere suggests that the nature of Sodom's offense was homosexual. Instead, Isaiah implies that it was hypocrisy and social injustice; Jeremiah that it was adultery, deceit, and general wickedness; and Ezekiel that it was arrogance, greed, and indifference to the poor.[7] Then Jesus himself (though Bailey does not mention this) on three separate occasions alluded to the inhabitants of Sodom and Gomorrah, declaring that it would be "more bearable" for them on the day of judgment than for those who reject his gospel.[8] Yet in all these references there is not even a whiff or rumor of homosexual malpractice! It is only when we reach the Palestinian pseudepigraphical writings of the second century B.C. that Sodom's sin is identified as unnatural sexual behavior.[9] And this finds a clear echo in the Book of Jude, in which it is said that "Sodom and Gomorrah and the surrounding towns gave themselves up to sexual immorality and perversion" (v. 7), and in the works of Philo and Josephus, Jewish writers who were shocked by the homosexual practices of Greek society.

Bailey handles the Gibeah story in the same way, for they are closely parallel. Another resident alien (this time an anonymous "old man") invites two strangers (not angels but a Levite and his concubine) into his home. Evil men surround the house and make the same demand as the Sodomites, that the visitor be brought out "so that we may know him." The owner of the house first begs them not to be so "vile" to his "guest" and then offers his daughter and the concubine to them instead. The sin of the men of Gibeah, it is again suggested, was not their proposal of homosexual intercourse but their violation of the laws of hospitality.

Although Bailey must have known that his reconstruction of both stories was at best tentative, he yet makes the exaggerated claim that "there is not the least reason to believe, as a matter of either historical fact or of revealed truth, that the city of Sodom and its neighbors were destroyed because of their homosexual practices."[10] Instead, the Christian tradition about "sodomy" was derived from late, apocryphal Jewish sources.

But Bailey's case is not convincing for a number of reasons:

1. The adjectives *wicked, vile,* and *disgraceful* (Gen. 18:7; Judg. 19:23) do not seem appropriate to describe a breach of hospitality;
2. the offer of women instead "does look as if there is some sexual connotation to the episode";[11]

3. although the verb *yāda'* is used in the Old Testament only ten times of sexual intercourse, Bailey omits to mention that six of these occurrences are in Genesis and one in the Sodom story itself about Lot's daughters, who had not "known" a man (v. 8);
4. for those of us who take the New Testament documents seriously, Jude's unequivocal reference to the "sexual immorality and perversion" of Sodom and Gomorrah (v. 7) cannot be dismissed as merely an error copied from Jewish pseudepigrapha.

To be sure, homosexual behavior was not Sodom's only sin; but according to Scripture it was certainly one of its sins, which brought down upon it the fearful judgment of God.

### The Leviticus Texts

The two texts in Leviticus belong to the Holiness Code, which is the heart of the book and which challenges the people of God to follow his laws and not copy the practices either of Egypt (where they used to live) or of Canaan (to which he was bringing them). These practices included sexual relations within the prohibited degrees, a variety of sexual deviations, child sacrifice, idolatry, and social injustice of different kinds. It is in this context that we must read the following two texts:

> "Do not lie with a man as one lies with a woman; that is detestable" (Lev. 18:22).
> "If a man lies with a man as one lies with a woman, both of them have done what is detestable. They must be put to death; their blood will be on their own heads" (Lev. 20:13).

"It is hardly open to doubt," writes Bailey, "that both the laws in Leviticus relate to ordinary homosexual acts between men, and not to ritual or other acts performed in the name of religion."[12] Others, however, affirm the very point which Bailey denies. They point out that the two texts are embedded in a context preoccupied largely with ritual cleanness, and Peter Coleman adds that the word translated "detestable" or "abomination" in both verses is associated with idolatry. "In English the word expresses disgust or disapproval, but in the Bible its predominant meaning is concerned with religious truth rather than morality or aesthetics."[13] Are these prohibitions merely religious taboos, then? Are they connected with that other prohibition, "No Israelite, man or woman, is to become a temple prostitute" (Deut. 23:17 TEV)? For certainly the

Canaanite fertility cult did include ritual prostitution and therefore provided both male and female "sacred prostitutes" (even if there is no clear evidence that either engaged in homosexual intercourse). The evil kings of Israel and Judah were constantly introducing them into the religion of Yahweh, and the righteous kings were constantly expelling them.[14] The homosexual lobby argues therefore that the Levitical texts prohibit religious practices which have long since ceased and have no relevance to homosexual partnerships today. The burden of proof is with them, however. The plain, natural interpretation of these two verses is that they prohibit homosexual intercourse of every kind. And the requirement of the death penalty (long since abrogated, of course) indicates the extreme seriousness with which homosexual practices were viewed.

## Paul's Teaching in Romans 1

Because of this, God gave them over to shameful lusts. Even their women exchanged natural relations for unnatural ones. In the same way the men also abandoned natural relations with women and were inflamed with lust for one another. Men committed indecent acts with other men, and received in themselves the due penalty for their perversion.

Romans 1:26–27

The Biblical Prohibitions

All are agreed that the apostle is describing idolatrous pagans in the Greco-Roman world of his day. They had a certain knowledge of God through the created universe (vv. 19–20) and their own moral sense (v. 32), yet they suppressed the truth they knew in order to practice wickedness. Instead of giving to God the honor due to him, they turned to idols, confusing the Creator with his creatures. In judgment upon them, "God gave them over" to their depraved minds and their decadent practices (vv. 24, 26, 28), including "unnatural" sex. It seems at first sight to be a definite condemnation of homosexual behavior. But two arguments are advanced on the other side. (1) Although Paul knew nothing of the modern distinction between "inverts" (who have a homosexual disposition) and "perverts" (who, though heterosexually inclined, indulge in homosexual practices), nevertheless it is the latter he is condemning, not the former. This must be so, it is urged, because they are described as having "abandoned" natural relations with women, whereas no exclusively homosexual male would ever have had them. (2) Paul is evidently portraying the reckless, shameless, profligate, promiscuous behavior of people whom God has judicially "given up"; what relevance has this to committed, loving homosexual partnerships? These two arguments can be rebutted, however; especially by the apos-

these words mean? To begin with, it is extremely unfortunate that in the original Revised Standard Version translation of 1 Corinthians 6:9 they were combined and translated "homosexuals." Bailey was right to protest, since the use of the word "inevitably suggests that the genuine invert, even though he be a man of irreproachable morals, is automatically branded as unrighteous and excluded from the Kingdom of God."[15] Fortunately, the revisers heeded the protest, and the second edition (1973), though still combining the words, rendered them "sexual perverts." The point is that all ten categories listed in 1 Corinthians 6:9–10 (with the possible exception of "the greedy") denote people who have offended by their *actions*—for example, idolaters, adulterers, and thieves.

The two Greek words *malakoi* and *arsenokoitai* should not be combined, however, since they "have precise meanings. The first is literally 'soft to the touch' and metaphorically, among the Greeks, meant males (not necessarily boys) who played the passive role in homosexual intercourse. The second means literally 'male in a bed,' and the Greeks used this expression to describe the one who took the active role."[16] The Jerusalem Bible follows James Moffatt in using the ugly words "catamites and sodomites," while among his conclusions Coleman suggests that "probably

Paul had commercial paederasty in mind between older men and post-pubertal boys, the most common pattern of homosexual behavior in the classical world."[17] If this is so, then once again it can be (and has been) argued that the Pauline condemnations are not relevant to homosexual adults who are both consenting and committed to one another. This is not, however, the conclusion which Coleman himself draws. His summary is as follows: "Taken together, St. Paul's writings repudiate homosexual behavior as a vice of the Gentiles in Romans, as a bar to the Kingdom in Corinthians, and as an offense to be repudiated by the moral law in 1 Timothy."[18]

## Moving beyond Proof Texts

Reviewing these biblical references to homosexual behavior, we have to agree that there are only four of them. Must we then conclude that the topic is marginal to the main thrust of the Bible? Must we further concede that they constitute a rather flimsy basis on which to take a firm stand against a homosexual lifestyle? Are those protagonists right who claim that the biblical prohibitions are "highly specific"[19]—against violations of hospitality (Sodom and Gibeah), against cultic taboos (Leviticus), against shameless orgies (Romans), and against male prostitution or the corruption of the young (1 Corinthians and 1 Timothy), and that none of these passages allude to, let alone condemns, a loving partnership between genuine homosexual inverts? This is the conclusion reached, for example, by Letha Scanzoni and Virginia Mollenkott in their book *Is the Homosexual My Neighbor?* They write: "The Bible clearly condemns certain kinds of homosexual practice (. . . gang rape, idolatry and lustful promiscuity). However, it appears to be silent in certain other aspects of homosexuality—both the 'homosexual orientation' and 'a committed love-relationship analogous to heterosexual monogamy.'"[20]

But no: Plausible as such a conclusion may sound, we cannot handle the biblical material in this way. The Christian rejection of homosexual practices does not rest on "a few isolated and obscure proof texts" (as is sometimes said) whose traditional explanation (it is further claimed) can be overthrown. And it is disturbing that those who write on this subject and include in their treatment a section on the biblical teaching all seem to deal with it in this way. For example, "Consideration of the Christian attitude to homosexual practices," writes Bailey, "inevitably begins with the story of the destruction of Sodom and Gomorrah."[21] But this beginning is not at all inevitable. In fact, it is positively mistaken.

For the *negative* prohibitions of homosexual practices in Scripture make sense only in the light of its *positive* teaching in Genesis 1 and 2 about human sexuality and heterosexual marriage. Yet Bailey's book contains no allusion to these chapters at all. And even Coleman, whose *Christian Attitudes to Homosexuality* is probably the most comprehensive biblical, historical, and moral survey which has yet been published, mentions them only in a passing reference to 1 Corinthians 6, where Paul quotes Genesis 2:24. Yet without the wholesome positive teaching of the Bible on sex and marriage, our perspective on the homosexual question is bound to be skewed.

# 3

# SEXUALITY
# AND MARRIAGE
# IN THE BIBLE

The essential place to begin our investigation, it seems to me, is the institution of marriage in Genesis 2. Since members of the Lesbian and Gay Christian Movement deliberately draw a parallel between heterosexual marriages and homosexual partnerships, it is necessary to ask whether this parallel can be justified.

## Fundamental Truths about Marriage

It is clear that in his providence God has given us two distinct accounts of creation. The first (Genesis 1) is general and affirms the equality of the sexes, since both share in the image of God and the stewardship of the earth. The second (Genesis 2) is particular and affirms the complementarity of the sexes, which constitutes the basis for heterosexual marriage. In this second account of creation, three fundamental truths emerge.

First, *the human need for companionship.* "It is not good for the man to be alone" (v. 18). True, this assertion is later qualified when the apostle Paul (surely echoing Genesis) writes, "It is good for a man not to marry" (1 Cor. 7:1). That is to say, although marriage is the good institution of God, the call to singleness is also the good vocation of some. Nevertheless, as a general rule, "It is not good for the man to be alone." For God has created us social beings. Since he is love and has made us in his own likeness, he has given us a capacity to love and be loved. He intends us to live in community, not in solitude. In particular, God continues, "I will make a helper suitable for him." Moreover, this "helper" or companion, whom God pronounces "suitable for him," is also to be his sexual partner, with whom he is to become "one flesh," so that they might thereby both consummate their love and conceive their children.

Secondly, Genesis 2 reveals *the divine provision to meet this human need.* Having affirmed Adam's need for a partner, the search for a suitable one begins. God first parades the birds and

Sexuality and Marriage in the Bible

beasts before him, and Adam proceeds to "name" them, to symbolize his taking them into his service. But "for Adam no suitable helper was found" (v. 20) who could live "alongside" or "opposite" him, who could be his complement, his counterpart, his companion, let alone his mate. So a special creation was necessary.

The debate about how literally we are intended to understand what follows (the divine surgery under a divine anesthetic) must not prevent us from grasping the point. Something happened during Adam's deep sleep. A special work of divine creation took place. The sexes became differentiated. Out of the undifferentiated humanity of Adam, male and female emerged. And Adam awoke from his deep sleep to behold before him a reflection of himself, a complement to himself, indeed a very part of himself. Next, having created the woman out of the man, God himself brought her to him, much as today the bride's father gives the bride away. And Adam broke spontaneously into history's first love poem, saying that now at last there stood before him a creature of such beauty in herself and similarity to him that she appeared to be (as indeed she was) "made for him":

> "This is now bone of my bones
> and flesh of my flesh;

She shall be called 'woman,'
for she was taken out of man."

verse 23

There can be no doubting the emphasis of this story. According to Genesis 1 Eve, like Adam, was created in the image of God. But as to the manner of her creation, according to Genesis 2, she was made neither out of nothing (like the universe), nor out of "the dust of the ground" (like Adam, v. 7), but out of Adam.

The third great truth of Genesis 2 concerns *the resulting institution of marriage*. Adam's love poem is recorded in verse 23. The "therefore" or "for this reason" of verse 24 is the narrator's deduction: "For this reason a man will leave his father and mother and be united to his wife, and they will become one flesh." Even the inattentive reader will be struck by the three references to flesh: "this is . . . flesh of my flesh"; "they will become one flesh." We may be certain that this is deliberate, not accidental. It teaches that heterosexual intercourse in marriage is more than a union; it is a kind of reunion. It is not a union of alien persons who do not belong to one another and cannot appropriately become one flesh. On the contrary, it is the union of two persons who originally were one, were then separated from each other, and now in the sexual encounter of marriage come together again.

It is surely this which explains the profound mystery of heterosexual intimacy, which poets and philosophers have celebrated in every culture. Heterosexual intercourse is much more than a union of bodies; it is a blending of complementary personalities through which, in the midst of prevailing alienation, the rich, created oneness of human being is experienced again. And the complementarity of male and female sexual organs is only a symbol at the physical level of a much deeper spiritual complementarity.

In order to become one flesh, however, and experience this sacred mystery, certain preliminaries are necessary, which are constituent parts of marriage. According to verse 24 (RSV), "Therefore a man [the singular indicates that marriage is an exclusive union between two individuals] leaves his father and his mother [a public social occasion is in view] and cleaves to his wife [marriage is a loving, cleaving commitment or covenant, which is heterosexual and permanent], and they become one flesh [for marriage must be consummated in sexual intercourse, which is a sign and seal of the marriage covenant and over which no shadow of shame or embarrassment had yet been cast (v. 25)]."

It is of the utmost importance to note that Jesus himself later endorsed this Old Testament definition of marriage. In doing so, he both introduced it with words from Genesis 1:27 (that the Creator "made them male and female" [Matt. 19:4]) and concluded it with his own comment ("so they are no longer two, but one. Therefore what God has joined together, let man not separate" [Matt. 19:6]). He thus made three statements about God the Creator's activity. First, God "made" them male and female. Secondly, God "said" that a man must leave his parents and cleave to his wife. Thirdly, he "joined" them together in such a way that no human being might put them apart. Here, then, are three truths which Jesus affirmed:

1. Heterosexual gender is a divine creation;
2. heterosexual marriage is a divine institution; and
3. heterosexual fidelity is the divine intention.

A homosexual liaison is a breach of all three of these divine purposes.

## Homosexuality and Marriage

It is in this context of the creation narratives of Genesis 1 and 2 that I need to respond to Michael

Vasey's sincere but misguided attempt, in his book *Strangers and Friends,* to combine evangelical faith with homosexual advocacy. In regard to his historical thesis that there was "widespread acceptance of homosexual desire and behavior among Christians until about the thirteenth century,"[22] he is dependent on the writings of John Boswell.[23] The scholarly assessment of Boswell's work by his fellow historians, however, has ranged "from the sharply critical to the dismissive to the devastating."[24] Dr. David Wright of Edinburgh University ends his article on homosexuality in *The Encyclopedia of Early Christianity* with these words: "The conclusion must be that, for all its interest and stimulus, Boswell's book provides at the end of the day not one firm piece of evidence that the teaching mind of the early church countenanced homosexual activity."[25]

Michael Vasey's handling of the biblical material is even less plausible. He virtually dismisses any appeal to the implications of Genesis 2:24 on the ground that "it imposes on scripture the domestic ideals of the nuclear family,"[26] isolated, self-contained, and self-centered. He evinces a surprising degree of hostility to marriage and the family, caricaturing them as destructive "idols" of modern society.[27] Jesus did not marry, he reminds us, and implies by this that he disapproved of marriage, for "it is precisely the passage in which Jesus quotes Genesis 2:24 that commends the renunciation of marriage."[28] Indeed, he suggests, there is a fundamental conflict between marriage and the gospel in the teaching of Jesus and his apostles. "For them the family was part of the present world order which was characterized by rebellion against God."[29] Hence "withdrawal from the social institutions and responsibilities of marriage and the family was a step into Christian freedom," so that people need not "continue as slaves within the present transient order."[30] In such an analysis the way is opened for homosexual partnerships as another, even a better, option.

But Michael Vasey has twisted the biblical material to suit his purpose. Neither Jesus' own singleness nor his teaching that singleness is a divine vocation for some (Matt. 19:11–12) may be taken as evidence that he opposed marriage and family, for they belong to the created order. Nor is the family envisaged in Genesis 1 and 2 "nuclear" in a negative or selfish sense. To be sure, Jesus did inaugurate a new order, refer to his new community as his family (Mark 3:34), and warn that if an unavoidable conflict arises between our loyalty to him and our loyalty to our natural family, then our loyalty to him takes precedence (Matt. 10:37; Luke 14:26). But Jesus and his apostles also insisted that Christians have a continuing obligation to their natural family,

Sexuality and Marriage in the Bible

including reciprocal duties between parents and children and between husbands and wives (e.g., Mark 7:9–13; Eph. 5:22–6:4). The new creation restores and redeems the old; it does not reject or replace it. As for idols, every good gift of God can become an idol, including marriage and family, but in themselves neither is idolatrous or enslaving. A homosexual partnership, however, is essentially incompatible with marriage as the God-ordained context for one-flesh intimacy.

Thus Scripture defines the marriage God instituted in terms of heterosexual monogamy. It is the union of one man with one woman, which must be publicly acknowledged (the leaving of parents), permanently sealed (he will "cleave to his wife"), and physically consummated ("one flesh"). And Scripture envisages no other kind of marriage or sexual intercourse, for God provided no alternative.

Christians should not therefore single out homosexual intercourse for special condemnation. The fact is that every kind of sexual relationship and activity which deviates from God's revealed intention is *ipso facto* displeasing to him and under his judgment. This includes polygamy and polyandry (which infringe the "one man, one woman" principle), cohabitation and clandestine unions (since these have involved no decisive public leaving of parents), casual encounters and tem-

# 4
# CONTEMPORARY ARGUMENTS CONSIDERED

Homosexual Christians are not, however, satisfied with this biblical teaching about human sexuality and the institution of heterosexual marriage. They bring forward a number of objections to it to defend the legitimacy of homosexual partnerships.

## The Argument about Scripture and Culture

Traditionally, it has been assumed that the Bible condemns all homosexual acts. But are the biblical writers reliable guides in this matter? Were their horizons not bounded by their own experience and culture? The cultural argument usually takes one of two forms.

First, the biblical authors were addressing themselves to questions relevant to their own circumstances, and these were very different from ours. In the Sodom and Gibeah stories they were preoccupied either with conventions of hospitality in the ancient Near East which are now obsolete, or (if the sin was sexual at all) with the extremely unusual phenomenon of homosexual gang rape. In the Levitical laws the concern was with antiquated fertility rituals, while Paul was addressing himself to the particular sexual preferences of Greek pederasts. It is all so antiquarian. The biblical authors' imprisonment in their own cultures renders their teaching on this topic irrelevant.

The second and complementary culture problem is that the biblical writers were not addressing themselves to *our* questions. Thus the problem of Scripture is not only with its teaching but also with its silence. Paul (let alone the Old Testament authors) knew nothing of post-Freudian psychology. They had never heard of "the homosexual condition"; they knew only about certain practices. The difference between "inversion" and "perversion" would have been incomprehensible to them. The very notion that two men or two women could fall in love with each other and develop a deeply loving, stable relationship comparable to marriage simply never entered their heads.

If the only biblical teaching on this topic were to be found in the prohibition texts, it might be difficult to answer these objections. But once those texts are seen in relation to the divine institution of marriage, we are in possession of a principle of divine revelation which is universally applicable. It was applicable to the cultural situations of both the ancient Near East and the first-century Greco-Roman world, and it is equally applicable to modern sexual questions of which the ancients were quite ignorant. The reason for the biblical prohibitions is the same reason why modern loving homosexual partnerships must also be condemned, namely that they are incompatible with God's created order (heterosexual monogamy). And since that order was established by creation, not culture, its validity is both permanent and universal. There can be no "liberation" from God's created norms; true liberation is found only in accepting them.

This argumentation is the opposite of the "biblical literalism" of which the gay lobby tends to accuse us. It is rather to look beneath the surface of the biblical prohibitions to the essential positives of divine revelation on sexuality and marriage. It is significant that those who are advocating same-sex partnerships usually omit Genesis 1 and 2 from their discussion, even though Jesus our Lord himself endorsed the teaching of those passages.

## The Argument about Creation and Nature

People sometimes make this kind of statement: "I'm gay because God made me that way. So gay must be good. I cannot believe that God would create people homosexual and then deny them the right to sexual self-expression. I intend, therefore, to affirm, and indeed celebrate, what I am by creation." Or again, "You may say that homosexual practice is against nature and normality; but it's not against *my* nature, nor is it in the slightest degree abnormal for *me*." Norman Pittenger was quite outspoken in his use of this argument a couple of decades ago. A homosexual person, he writes, is "not an 'abnormal' person with 'unnatural' desires and habits." On the contrary, "a heterosexually oriented person acts 'naturally' when he acts heterosexually, while a homosexually oriented person acts equally 'naturally' when he acts in accordance with his basic, inbuilt homosexual desire and drive."[31]

Others argue that homosexual behavior is "natural" (1) because in many primitive societies it is fairly acceptable, (2) because in some advanced civilizations (ancient Greece, for example) it was even idealized, and (3) because it is said to be quite widespread in animals. Yet, according to Thomas E. Schmidt, the research consensus is that "no evidence has as yet emerged to suggest that any non-human primate . . . would rate a 6 (exclusively homosexual) on the Kinsey scale."[32]

In any case, these arguments express an extremely subjective view of what is natural and normal. We should not accept Norman Pittenger's statement that there are "no eternal standards of normality or naturalness."[33] Nor can we agree that animal behavior sets standards for human behavior! For God has established a norm for sex and marriage by creation. This was already recognized in the Old Testament era. Thus, sexual relations with an animal were forbidden because "that is a perversion" (Lev. 18:23), in other words a violation or confusion of nature, which indicates an "embryonic sense of natural law."[34] The same verdict is passed on Sodom by the second century B.C. *Testament of Naphtali:* "As the sun and the stars do not change their order, so the tribe of Naphtali are to obey God rather than the disorderliness of idolatry. Recognizing in all created things the Lord who made them, they are not to become as Sodom, which changed the order of nature."[35]

The same concept was clearly in Paul's mind in Romans 1. When he writes of women who had "exchanged natural relations for unnatural ones" and of men who had "abandoned natural relations," he means by "nature" *(physis)* the natural order of things which God has established (as in 2:14, 27 and 11:24). What Paul is condemning, therefore, is not the perverted behavior of heterosexual people who were acting against *their* nature, as Boswell argues,[36] but any human behavior which is against "Nature," that is, against God's created order. Richard B. Hays has written a thorough rebuttal of Boswell's exegesis of Romans 1. He provides ample contemporary evidence that the opposition of "natural" *(kata physin)* and "unnatural" *(para physin)* was "very frequently used . . . as a way of distinguishing between heterosexual and homosexual behavior."[37]

British commentators confirm his conclusion. As C. K. Barrett puts it, "In the obscene pleasures to which he [Paul] refers is to be seen precisely that perversion of the created order which may be expected when men put the creation in place of the Creator."[38] Similarly, Charles Cranfield writes that by "natural" and "unnatural" "Paul clearly means 'in accordance with the intention of the Creator' and 'contrary to the intention of the Creator,' respectively." Again, "the decisive factor in Paul's use of it [*physis*, 'nature'] is his biblical doctrine of creation. It denotes that order which is manifest in God's creation and which men have no excuse for failing to recognize and respect."[39]

An appeal to the created order should also be our response to another argument which is being developed by a few people today, especially in the Church of England. They point out that the early church distinguished between primary and secondary issues, insisting on agreement about the former but allowing freedom to disagree about the latter. The two examples of Christian liberty which they usually quote are circumcision and idol meats. They then draw a parallel with homosexual practice, suggesting that it is a second-order issue in which we can give one another freedom. But actually the early church was more subtle in its argumentation than they allow. The Jerusalem Council (Acts 15) decreed that circumcision was definitely not necessary for salvation (a first order question) but allowed its continuance as a matter of policy or culture (second order). The council also decided that, although of course idolatry was forbidden (first order), eating idol meats was not necessarily idolatrous, so that Christians with a strong, educated conscience might eat them (second order). Thus the second-order issues, in which Christian liberty was allowed, were neither theological nor moral but cultural. But this is not the case with homosexual practice.

A second parallel is sometimes drawn. When the debate over women's ordination was at its height, the General Synod of the Church of England agreed that the church should not be obliged to choose between the two positions (for and against), declaring one to be right and the other wrong, but should rather preserve unity by recognizing both to have integrity. In consequence, we are living with "the two integrities." Why, it is asked, should we not equally acknowledge "two integrities" in relation to same-sex partnerships and not force people to choose? The answer should be clear. Even if women's ordination is a second-order issue (which many would deny), homosexual partnerships are not. Gender in relation to marriage is a much more fundamental matter than gender in relation to ministry. For marriage has been recognized as a heterosexual union from the beginning of God's creation and institution; it is basic to human society as God intended it, and its biblical basis is incontrovertible. Dr. Wolfhart Pannenberg, professor of theology at Munich University, is outspoken on this subject. Having declared that "the biblical assessments of homosexual practice are unambiguous in their rejection," he concludes that a church which were to recognize homosexual unions as equivalent to marriage "would cease to be the one, holy, catholic, and apostolic church."[40]

# The Argument about Quality of Relationships

The Lesbian and Gay Christian Movement borrows from Scripture the truth that love is the greatest thing in the world (which it is) and from the "new morality" or "situation ethics" of the 1960s the notion that love is an adequate criterion by which to judge every relationship (which it is not). Yet this view is gaining ground today. One of the first official documents to embrace it was the Friends' report *Towards a Quaker View of Sex* (1963). It included the statements "one should no more deplore 'homosexuality' than left-handedness"[41] and "surely it is the nature and quality of a relationship that matters."[42] Similarly, in 1979 the Methodist Church's Division of Social Responsibility, in its report *A Christian Understanding of Human Sexuality,* argued that "homosexual activities" are "not intrinsically wrong," since "the quality of any homosexual relationship is . . . to be assessed by the same basic criteria which have been applied to heterosexual relationships. For homosexual men and women, permanent relationships characterized by love can be an appropriate and Christian way of expressing their sexuality."[43] The same year, an Anglican working party issued the report *Homosexual Relationships: A Contribution to Discus-*

*sion*. It was more cautious, judicious, and ambivalent than the Quaker and Methodist reports. Its authors did not feel able to repudiate centuries of Christian tradition, yet they "did not think it possible to deny" that in some circumstances individuals may "justifiably choose" a homosexual relationship in their search for companionship and sexual love "similar" to those found in marriage.[44]

In his *Time for Consent* Pittenger lists what he sees to be the six characteristics of a truly loving relationship. They are

1. commitment (the free self-giving of each to the other),
2. mutuality in giving and receiving (a sharing in which each finds his or her self in the other),
3. tenderness (no coercion or cruelty),
4. faithfulness (the intention of a lifelong relationship),
5. hopefulness (each serving the other's maturity), and
6. desire for union.[45]

If, then, a homosexual relationship, whether between two men or two women, is characterized by these qualities of love, surely (the argument runs) it must be affirmed as good and not rejected as evil. For it rescues people from loneliness, selfishness, and promiscuity. It can be just as rich and responsible, as liberating and fulfilling, as a heterosexual marriage.

More recently, in the spring of 1997, in a lecture delivered in London at St. Martin in the Fields, Bishop John Austin Baker gave his own version of this argument. Formerly Bishop of Salisbury, chairman of the Church of England's Doctrine Commission, and chairman of the drafting group which produced the moderate report *Issues in Human Sexuality* (1991), Bishop Baker astonished the church by his apparent change of mind. The goal of Christian discipleship, he rightly affirmed, is "Christlikeness," that is, "a creative living out of the values, priorities and attitudes that marked his humanity," especially of love. Now sex in marriage can be "a true making of love," and "erotic love can and often does have the same beneficial effects in the life of same-sex couples."

There are three reasons, however, why this claim for the quality of same-sex love is flawed. First, the concept of lifelong, quasi-marital fidelity in homosexual partnerships is largely a myth, a theoretical ideal which is contradicted by the facts. The truth is that gay relationships are characterized more by promiscuity than by fidelity. A number of researches have been made.

"One of the most carefully researched studies of the most stable homosexual pairs," writes Dr. Jeffrey Satinover, "was researched and written by two authors who are themselves a homosexual couple." They found that "of the 156 couples studied, only seven had maintained sexual fidelity; of the hundred couples that had been together for more than five years, none had been able to maintain sexual fidelity." They added that "the expectation for outside sexual activity was the rule for male couples and the exception for heterosexuals."[46] The result of these research studies led Thomas Schmidt to conclude: "promiscuity among homosexual men is not a mere stereotype, and it is not merely the majority experience—it is virtually the *only* experience. . . . In short, there is practically no comparison possible to heterosexual marriage in terms of either fidelity or longevity. Tragically, lifelong faithfulness is almost non-existent in the homosexual experience."[47] There seems to be something inherently unstable about homosexual partnerships. The quality of relationships argument does not hold water.

Secondly, it is difficult to maintain that homosexual partnerships are just as much an expression of love as heterosexual marriages in the light of the known damage and danger involved in usual gay sexual practices. Dr. Satinover has the courage to give us "the brute facts about the adverse consequences of homosexuality" based on the most recent medical studies. He writes of infectious hepatitis, which increases the risk of liver cancer, of frequently fatal rectal cancer, and of a twenty-five- to thirty-year decrease in life expectancy.[48] Thomas Schmidt is even more explicit, describing seven nonviral and four viral infections which are transmitted by oral and anal sex. It is true that some diseases can also be transmitted by similar activity between heterosexual people, but "these health problems are rampant in the homosexual population because they are easily spread by promiscuity and by most of the practices favored by homosexuals." And these diseases are apart from AIDS, to which we will come shortly. Dr. Schmidt justly calls this chapter "The Price of Love."[49] If these physical dangers attend common gay sexual activities, can authentic lovers engage in them?

But, thirdly, the biblical Christian cannot accept the basic premise on which this case rests, namely that love is the only absolute, that besides it all moral law has been abolished, and that whatever seems to be compatible with love is *ipso facto* good, irrespective of all other considerations. This cannot be so. For love needs law to guide it. In emphasizing love for God and neighbor as the two great commandments, Jesus and his apostles did not discard all other commandments. On the contrary, Jesus says, "If you love me, you will keep my commandments" (John 14:15 NRSV), and Paul writes, "Love is the fulfilling [not the abrogating] of the law" (Rom. 13:8 NRSV).

So, then, although the loving quality of a relationship is an essential, it is not by itself a sufficient criterion to authenticate it. For example, if love were the only test of authenticity, there would be nothing against polygamy, for a polygamist could certainly enjoy with several mates relationships which reflect all of Pittenger's six characteristics. Or let me give you a better illustration, drawn from my own pastoral experience. On several different occasions a married man has told me that he has fallen in love with another woman. When I have gently remonstrated with him, he has responded in words like these: "Yes, I agree, I already have a wife and family. But this new relationship is the real thing. We were made for each other. Our love for each other has a quality and depth we have never known before. It *must* be right." But no, I have had to say to him, it is not right. No man is justified in breaking his marriage covenant with his wife on the ground that the quality of his love for another woman is richer. Quality of love is not the only yardstick by which to measure what is good or right.

54

Similarly, we should not deny that homosexual relationships can be loving (although *a priori* they cannot attain the same richness as the heterosexual complementarity which God has ordained). As the 1994 Ramsey Colloquium statement puts it, "even a distorted love retains traces of love's grandeur."[50] But the love quality of gay relationships is not sufficient to justify them. Indeed, I have to add that they are incompatible with true love because they are incompatible with God's law. Love is concerned for the highest welfare of the beloved. And our highest human welfare is found in obedience to God's law and purpose, not in revolt against them.

Some leaders of the Lesbian and Gay Christian Movement appear to be following the logic of their own position, for they are saying that even monogamy could be abandoned in the interests of "love." Malcolm Macourt, for example, has written that the Gay Liberationist's vision is of "a wide variety of life patterns," each of which is "held in equal esteem in society." Among them he lists the following alternatives: monogamy and multiple partnerships; partnerships for life and partnerships for a period of mutual growth; same-sex partners and opposite-sex partners; living in community and living in small family units.[51] There seem to be no limits to what some people seek to justify in the name of love.

Contemporary Arguments Considered

# The Argument about Justice and Rights

If some argue for homosexual partnerships on the basis of the love involved, others do so on the basis of justice. Desmond Tutu, for example, formerly Archbishop of Cape Town and universally admired for his courageous stand against apartheid and for racial equality, has several times said that for him the homosexual question is a simple matter of justice. Others agree. The justice argument runs like this: "Just as we may not discriminate between persons on account of their gender, color, ethnicity, or class, so we may not discriminate between persons on account of their sexual preference. For the God of the Bible is the God of justice, who is described as loving justice and hating injustice. Therefore the quest for justice must be a paramount obligation of the people of God. Now that slaves, women, and blacks have been liberated, gay liberation is long overdue. What civil rights activists were in the 1950s and '60s, gay rights activists are today. We should support them in their cause and join them in their struggle."

The vocabulary of oppression, liberation, rights, and justice, however, needs careful definition. "Gay liberation" presupposes an oppression from which homosexual people need to be set free, and "gay rights" implies that homosex-

Contemporary Arguments Considered

ual people are suffering a wrong which should be righted. But what is this oppression, this wrong, this injustice? If it is that they are being despised and rejected by sections of society on account of their sexual inclination, are in fact victims of homophobia, then indeed they have a grievance which must be redressed. For God opposes such discrimination and requires us to love and respect all human beings without distinction. If, on the other hand, the "wrong" or "injustice" complained of is society's refusal to recognize homosexual partnerships as a legitimate alternative to heterosexual marriages, then talk of "justice" is inappropriate, since human beings may not claim as a "right" what God has not given them.

The analogy between gays and the liberation of slaves, blacks, and women is inexact and misleading. In each case we need to clarify the Creator's original intention. Thus, in spite of misguided attempts to justify slavery and racism from Scripture, both are fundamentally incompatible with the created equality of human beings. Similarly, the Bible honors womanhood by affirming that men and women share equally in the image of God and the stewardship of the environment, and its teaching on masculine "headship" or responsibility may not be interpreted as contradicting this equality. But sexual intercourse belongs, according to the plain teaching of Scripture, to heterosexual marriage alone. Therefore homosexual intercourse cannot be regarded as a permissible equivalent, let alone a divine right. True gay liberation (like all authentic liberation) is not freedom from God's revealed purpose in order to construct our own morality; it is rather freedom from our self-willed rebellion in order to love and obey him.

## The Argument about Acceptance and the Gospel

"Surely," some people are saying, "it is the duty of heterosexual Christians to accept homosexual Christians. Paul told us to accept—indeed, welcome—one another. If God has welcomed somebody, who are we to pass judgment on him (Rom. 14:1ff; 15:7)?" Pittenger goes further and declares that those who reject homosexual people "have utterly failed to understand the Christian gospel." We do not receive the grace of God because we are good and confess our sins, he continues; it is the other way around. "It's always God's grace which comes *first* . . . his forgiveness awakens our repentance."[52] He even quotes the hymn "Just as I Am" and adds, "the whole point of the Christian gospel is that God loves and accepts us just as we are."[53]

This is a very confused statement of the gospel, however. God does indeed accept us just as we are, and we do not have to make ourselves good first; indeed, we cannot. But his "acceptance" means that he fully and freely forgives all who repent and believe, not that he condones our continuance in sin. Again, it is true that we must accept one another, but only as fellow penitents and fellow pilgrims, not as fellow sinners who are resolved to persist in our sinning. Michael Vasey makes much of the fact that Jesus was called (and was) "the friend of sinners." And indeed his offer of friendship to sinners like us is truly wonderful. But he welcomes us in order to redeem and transform us, not to leave us alone in our sins. No acceptance, either by God or by the church, is promised to us if we harden our hearts against God's Word and will. Only judgment.

# 5
# THE AIDS EPIDEMIC

Is AIDS, then, the judgment of God on practicing homosexual men? This is what some evangelical Christians have confidently declared and is the reason why I have included a section on AIDS. Before we are in a position to decide, however, we need to know the basic facts.

AIDS (Acquired Immune Deficiency Syndrome) was identified and described for the first time in 1981 in the United States. It is spread through HIV (Human Immunodeficiency Virus), which may then lie dormant and unsuspected in its human host for ten years or even longer. But eventually it will in most cases manifest itself by attacking and damaging the body's immune and nervous systems, so making the body defenseless against certain fatal diseases. The origin of this human virus is unknown, although the accepted wisdom is that it developed as the spontaneous mutation of a virus which had long infected African monkeys.

## Myths about AIDS

Many myths surround AIDS (especially in relation to its transmission and its extent), which need to be dispelled.

First, AIDS is not an easily caught infectious disease. The virus is transmitted only in body fluids, particularly in semen and blood. The commonest ways of getting it are through sexual intercourse with an infected partner, through a transfusion of contaminated blood, and through an injection with an unsterilized needle (the sharing of needles by drug addicts is a dangerous practice). A child in the womb is also greatly at risk if the pregnant mother is HIV positive.

Secondly, AIDS is not a specifically "gay plague." It was given that inaccurate designation in the early 1980s because it first appeared in the male homosexual communities of San Francisco and New York. But the virus is transmitted by heterosexual as well as homosexual intercourse (overwhelmingly so in Africa, where homosexual behavior is almost unknown), and AIDS sufferers include many women and babies as well as men.

It is promiscuous sexual behavior which spreads the disease most rapidly; whether this takes place with same-sex or opposite-sex partners is largely irrelevant. "The greater the numbers, the greater the risk," writes Dr. Patrick Dixon, founder of ACET (AIDS Care Education and Training), whose well-researched and compassionate book *The Truth about AIDS* I recommend.[54]

Thirdly, AIDS is not a peculiarly western phenomenon. It seemed in the early eighties to be so, because American and European hospitals, possessing the necessary resources, were the first to diagnose it. But it is increasingly a worldwide disease. In East and Central Africa it has reached epidemic proportions.

Fourthly, AIDS is not a problem which can be quickly solved. It is an incurable disease, with neither preventive vaccine nor therapeutic drug in sight. The drug known as AZT can prolong an AIDS victim's life by about a year and alleviate suffering, but it has unpleasant side effects and is a treatment, not a cure. Meanwhile, the statistics are growing at an alarming rate. The American Psychiatric Association Press reports that "30% of all 20-year-old gay men will be HIV positive or dead of AIDS by the time they are age 30."[55] In 1996 alone there were an estimated 3.1 million new HIV infections around the world. In sub-Saharan Africa there are fourteen million people living with HIV/AIDS. In parts of East Africa, over 10 percent of women attending prenatal clinics are HIV infected, with some clinics reporting numbers over 40 percent. Almost one million children in Kenya, Rwanda, Uganda, and Zambia have been orphaned as a result of AIDS, with approximately 8 percent of these children infected themselves. AIDS is also spreading with incredible ferocity in some parts of India; with up to 10 percent of truck drivers infected, it is moving beyond the urban centers and into the countryside. The ten thousand estimated cases of HIV infection in China in 1993 increased to 100,000 in 1995. But the most appalling figure of all was given in a 1997 joint report by the United Nations and the World Health Organization. Confessing that the scale of the global epidemic had been "grossly underestimated," the report reckoned that the total number of people living with HIV/AIDS was then more than thirty million and would reach forty million by A.D. 2000.[56]

Fifthly, AIDS cannot be avoided merely by the use of a condom, which is known to be an unreliable contraceptive. Dr. Dixon sums the matter up succinctly: "Condoms do not make sex safe, they simply make it safer. Safe sex is sex between two partners who are not infected! This means a lifelong, faithful partnership between two people who were virgins and who now remain faithful to each other for life."[57] Or to quote the United States Catholic Conference, "abstinence outside of marriage and fidelity within marriage, as well as the avoidance of intravenous drug abuse, are the only morally correct and medically sure ways to prevent the spread of AIDS."[58]

## A Christian Response to AIDS

A threefold Christian response to these sobering facts and figures would seem to be appropriate.

First, *theological*. Reverting to the question of whether AIDS is a divine judgment on practicing homosexual men, I think we have to answer yes and no. No because Jesus warned us not to interpret calamities as God's specific judgments upon evil people (Luke 13:1–5). No also because AIDS victims include many women, especially faithful married women who have been infected by their unfaithful husbands, with a substantial minority of innocent hemophiliacs and children. But yes in the sense that Paul means when he writes: "Do not deceive yourselves; no one makes a fool of God. A person will reap exactly what he plants" (Gal. 6:7 TEV). The fact that we reap what we plant, or that evil actions bring evil consequences, seems to have been written by God into the ordering of his moral world. Christians cannot regard it as an accident, for example, that promiscuity exposes people to venereal diseases, that heavy smoking can lead to lung cancer, excessive alcohol to liver disorders, and overeating (directly or indirectly) to heart conditions. Moreover, this cause-and-effect mechanism is viewed in Scripture as one of the ways in which God's "wrath," that is, his just judgment on evil, is revealed (Rom. 1:18–32). Before the day of judgment arrives, Jesus taught, a process of judgment is already taking place (John 3:18–21; 5:24–29). AIDS may rightly be seen, then, as "part of God's judgment on society." "It is calling the bluff of the permissive society that there is any such thing as sexual liberation in promiscuity."[59]

Our second Christian response must be *pastoral*. We do not deny that many people have contracted AIDS as a result of their own sexual promiscuity. But this provides us with no possible justification for shunning or neglecting them, any more than we would those who damage themselves through drunken driving or other forms of recklessness. As the American Roman Catholic bishops have put it, "Stories of persons with AIDS must not become occasions for stereotyping or prejudice, for anger or recrimination, for rejection or isolation, for injustice or condemnation." Instead, "they provide us with an opportunity to walk with those who are suffering, to be compassionate towards those whom we might otherwise fear, to bring strength and courage both to those who face the prospect of dying as well as to their loved ones."[60] "Don't judge me," an American AIDS patient called Jerome said. "I'm living under my own judgment. What I need is for you to walk with me."[61] Local churches need especially to reach out to AIDS sufferers in their own fellowship and in their wider community. The Terrence Higgins Trust, named after the first person in Britain who is known to have died of AIDS (in 1982), teaches high standards of counseling and care, especially through the "buddy" service of volunteers which it has pioneered.[62] At the same time, we may be thankful that both the origins of the hospice movement and its extension from terminal cancer patients to AIDS victims have been due largely to Christian initiatives.[63]

Our third response must be *educational*. It is true that some people scorn this as a hopelessly inadequate reaction to the AIDS crisis and propose instead the compulsory isolation of all virus carriers. But the Christian conscience shrinks from such a ruthless measure, even if it could be democratically accepted and successfully imposed. Mandatory regular screening is also advocated by some, and the arguments for and against were well developed by Dr. David Cook in his 1989 London Lectures entitled *Just Health*.[64] But Christians are likely to prefer a thoroughgoing educational program as the most human and Christian way to combat ignorance, prejudice, fear, and promiscuous behavior and so turn back the AIDS tide. Certainly the current complacency and indifference, which are helping to spread the disease, can be overcome only by the relentless force of the facts. Dr. Dixon, in his "Ten Point Plan for the Government," urges that they "get an army of health educators on the road" to visit and address all the country's schools and colleges, factories and shops, clubs and pubs. In such a preventive educational program, the churches should have a major role. Is it not the failure of the churches to teach and exemplify God's standards of sexual morality which, more than anything else, is to blame for the current crisis?[65] We must not fail again but rather challenge society to sexual self-control and faithfulness and point to Jesus as the source of forgiveness and power. Several Christian groups have been set up to alert the churches to their responsibilities, to provide educational resources, and to encourage support groups.[66]

Above all, "the AIDS crisis challenges us profoundly to be the Church in deed and in truth: *to be the Church as a healing community.*" Indeed, because of our tendency to self-righteousness, "the healing community itself will need to be healed by the forgiveness of Christ."[67]

# 6

# FAITH, HOPE, AND LOVE

If homosexual practice must be regarded, in the light of the whole biblical revelation, not as a variant within the wide range of accepted normality but as a deviation from God's norm, and if we should therefore call homosexually inclined people to abstain from homosexual practices and partnerships, what advice and help can we give to encourage them to respond to this call? I would like to take Paul's triad of faith, hope, and love and apply it to homosexually inclined people.

## The Christian Call to Faith

Faith is our human response to divine revelation; it is believing God's Word.

First, *faith accepts God's standards.* The only alternative to heterosexual marriage is singleness and sexual abstinence. I think I know the implications of this. Nothing has helped me to understand the pain of homosexual celibacy more than Alex Davidson's moving book *The Returns of Love.* He writes of "this incessant tension between law and lust," "this monster that lurks in the depths," this "burning torment."[68]

The secular world says: "Sex is essential to human fulfillment. To expect homosexual people to abstain from homosexual practice is to condemn them to frustration and to drive them to neurosis, despair, and even suicide. It's outrageous to ask them to deny themselves what to them is a normal and natural mode of sexual expression. It's 'inhuman and inhumane.'[69] Indeed, it's positively cruel."

But no, the teaching of the Word of God is different. Sexual experience is not essential to human fulfillment. To be sure, it is a good gift of God. But it is not given to all, and it is not indispensable to humanness. People in Paul's day were saying that it was. Their slogan was "Food for the stomach and the stomach for food; sex for the body and the body for sex" (see 1 Cor. 6:13). But this is a lie of the devil. Jesus Christ was single yet perfect in his humanity. So it is possible to be single and human at the same time! Besides, God's

Faith, Hope, and Love

commands are good and not grievous. The yoke of Christ brings rest, not turmoil; conflict comes only to those who resist it.

At the very center of Christian discipleship is our participation in the death and resurrection of Jesus Christ. "The Saint Andrew's Day Statement" on the homosexuality debate (1995), commissioned by the Church of England Evangelical Council, emphasized this. We are "called to follow in the way of the cross." For "we all are summoned to various forms of self-denial. The struggle against disordered desires, or the misdirection of innocent desire, is part of every Christian's life, consciously undertaken in baptism." But after struggle comes victory; out of death, resurrection.[70]

So ultimately it is a crisis of faith: Whom shall we believe? God or the world? Shall we submit to the lordship of Jesus, or succumb to the pressures of prevailing culture? The true "orientation" of Christians is not what we are by constitution (hormones), but what we are by choice (heart, mind, and will).

Secondly, *faith accepts God's grace*. Abstinence is not only good, if God calls us to celibacy, but also possible. Many deny it, however. "You know the imperious strength of our sex drive," they say. "To ask us to control ourselves is just unreasonable." It is "so near to an impossibility," writes Pittenger, "that it's hardly worth talking about."[71]

Really? What then are we to make of Paul's statement following his warning to the Corinthians that male prostitutes and homosexual offenders will not inherit God's kingdom? "And that is what some of you were," he cries. "But you were washed, you were sanctified, you were justified in the name of the Lord Jesus Christ and by the Spirit of our God" (1 Cor. 6:11). And what shall we say to the millions of heterosexual people who are single? To be sure, all unmarried people experience the pain of struggle and loneliness. But how can we call ourselves Christians and declare that chastity is impossible? It is made harder by the sexual obsession of contemporary society. And we make it harder for ourselves if we listen to the world's plausible arguments, or lapse into self-pity, or feed our imagination with pornographic material and so inhabit a fantasy world in which Christ is not Lord, or ignore his command about plucking out our eyes and cutting off our hands and feet, that is, being ruthless with the avenues of temptation. But whatever our "thorn in the flesh" may be, Christ comes to us as he came to Paul and says, "My grace is sufficient for you, for my power is made perfect in weakness" (2 Cor. 12:9). To deny this is to portray Christians as the helpless victims of the world, the flesh, and the devil, to demean them into being less than human, and to contradict the gospel of God's grace.

Faith, Hope, and Love

# The Christian Call to Hope

I have said nothing so far about "healing" for homosexual people, understood now not as self-mastery but as the reversal of their sexual bias. Our expectation of this possibility will depend largely on our understanding of the cause or origin of the homosexual condition, and no final agreement on this has yet been reached. Many studies have been conducted, but they have failed to establish a single cause, whether inherited or learned. So scholars have tended to turn to theories of multiple causation, combining a biological predisposition (genetic and hormonal) with cultural and moral influences, childhood environment and experience, and repeatedly reinforced personal choices. Dr. Satinover concludes his investigation with an appeal to common sense: "One's character traits are in part innate, but are subject to modification by experience and choice."[72] So if homosexuality is at least partly learned, can it be unlearned?

Just as opinions differ on the causes of homosexuality, so they also differ on the possibilities and the means of "cure." This issue divides people into three categories: those who consider healing unnecessary, those who consider it possible, and those who consider it impossible.

First, we have to recognize that many homosexual people categorically reject the language of "cure" and "healing." They see no need (and have no wish) to change. Their position has been summed up in three convictions: Biologically, their condition is innate (being inherited); psychologically, it is irreversible; sociologically, it is normal.[73] They regard it as a great victory that in 1973 the trustees of the American Psychiatric Association removed homosexuality from its official list of mental illnesses. Michael Vasey declares that this decision was not the result of some "liberal" conspiracy.[74] But that is exactly what it was. Seventy years of psychiatric opinion were overthrown not by science (for no fresh evidence was produced) but by politics.[75] At least the Roman Catholic Church was neither impressed nor convinced. The American bishops in their 1986 "Pastoral Letter" continued to describe homosexuality as "intrinsically disordered" (par. 3).

Secondly, there are those who regard "healing," understood as the reversal of sexual orientation, as impossible. "No known method of treatment or punishment," writes D. J. West, "offers hope of making any substantial reduction in the vast army of adults practicing homosexuality"; it would be "more realistic to find room for them in society." He pleads for "tolerance," though not for "encouragement," of homosexual behavior.[76]

Are not these views, however, the despairing opinions of the secular mind? They challenge us

74                                    Faith, Hope, and Love

to articulate the third position, which is to believe that at least some degree of change is possible. Christians know that the homosexual condition, being a deviation from God's norm, is not a sign of created order but of fallen disorder. How, then, can we acquiesce in it or declare it incurable? We cannot. The only question is when and how we are to expect the divine deliverance and restoration to take place. The fact is that though Christian claims of homosexual "healings" are made, either through regeneration or through a subsequent work of the Holy Spirit, it is not easy to substantiate them.[77]

Martin Hallett, who before his conversion was active in the gay scene, has written a very honest account of his experience of what he calls "Christ's way out of homosexuality." He is candid about his continuing vulnerability, his need for safeguards, his yearning for love, and his occasional bouts of emotional turmoil. I am glad he entitled his autobiographical sketch, *I Am Learning to Love,* in the present tense, and subtitled it *A Personal Journey to Wholeness in Christ.* His final paragraph begins: "I have learnt; I am learning; I will learn to love God, other people and myself. This healing process will only be complete when I am with Jesus."[78]

True Freedom Trust has published a pamphlet entitled *Testimonies.* In it homosexual Christian men and women bear witness to what Christ has done for them. They have found a new identity in him and have a new sense of personal fulfillment as children of God. They have been delivered from guilt, shame, and fear by God's forgiving acceptance, and have been set free from thralldom to their former homosexual lifestyle by the indwelling power of the Holy Spirit. But they have not been delivered from their homosexual inclination, and therefore some inner pain continues alongside their new joy and peace. Here are two examples: "My prayers were not answered in the way I had hoped for, but the Lord greatly blessed me in giving me two Christian friends who lovingly accepted me for what I was." "After I was prayed over with the laying on of hands a spirit of perversion left me. I praise God for the deliverance I found that afternoon. . . . I can testify to over three years of freedom from homosexual activity. But I have not changed into a heterosexual in that time." Similar testimonies are given by ex-gay ministries in the United States. Over two hundred of them belong to the coalition called Exodus International.[79] Tim Stafford describes in a 1989 edition of *Christianity Today* his investigation into several of them. His conclusion is one of "cautious optimism." What ex-gays were claiming was "not a quick 180-degree reversal of their sexual desires"

Faith, Hope, and Love

but rather "a gradual reversal in their spiritual understanding of themselves as men and women in relationship to God." And this new self-understanding was "helping them to relearn distorted patterns of thinking and relating. They presented themselves as people in process."[80]

Is there really, then, no hope of a substantial change of inclination? Dr. Elizabeth Moberly believes there is. She has been led by her researches to the view that "a homosexual orientation does not depend on a genetic predisposition, hormonal imbalance, or abnormal learning process, but on difficulties in the parent-child relationships, especially in the earlier years of life." The "underlying principle," she continues, is "that the homosexual—whether man or woman—has suffered from some deficit in the relationship with the parent *of the same sex;* and that there is a corresponding drive to make good this deficit through the medium of same-sex or 'homosexual' relationships."[81] The deficit and the drive go together. The reparative drive for same-sex love is not itself pathological, but "quite the opposite—it is the attempt to resolve and heal the pathology." "The homosexual condition does not involve abnormal needs, but normal needs that have, abnormally, been left unmet in the ordinary process of growth." Homosexuality "is essentially a state of incomplete development" or of unmet needs.[82] So the proper solution is "the meeting of same-sex needs without sexual activity," for to eroticize growth deficits is to confuse emotional needs with physiological desires.[83] How, then, can these needs be met? The needs are legitimate, but what are the legitimate means of meeting them? Dr. Moberly's answer is that "substitute relationships for parental care are in God's redemptive plan, just as parental relationships are in his creative plan."[84] What is needed is deep, loving, lasting, same-sex but nonsexual relationships, especially in the church. "Love," she concludes, "both in prayer and in relationships, is the basic therapy. . . . Love is the basic problem, the great need, and the only true solution. If we are willing to seek and to mediate the healing and redeeming love of Christ, then healing for the homosexual will become a great and glorious reality."[85]

Even then, however, complete healing of body, mind, and spirit will not take place in this life. Some degree of deficit or disorder remains in each of us. But not forever! For the Christian's horizons are not bounded by this world. Jesus Christ is coming again; our bodies are going to be redeemed; sin, pain, and death are going to be abolished; and both we and the universe are going to be transformed. Then we shall be finally liberated from everything which defiles or distorts our personality. And this Christian assurance helps us to bear whatever our present pain may be. For

Faith, Hope, and Love

pain there is, in the midst of peace. "We know that the whole creation has been groaning as in the pains of childbirth right up to the present time. Not only so, but we ourselves, who have the first-fruits of the Spirit, groan inwardly as we wait eagerly for our adoption as sons, the redemption of our bodies" (Rom. 8:22–23). Thus our groans express the birthpangs of the new age. We are convinced that "our present sufferings are not worth comparing with the glory that will be revealed in us" (Rom. 8:18). This confident hope sustains us.

Alex Davidson derives comfort in the midst of his homosexuality from his Christian hope. "Isn't it one of the most wretched things about this condition," he writes, "that when you look ahead, the same impossible road seems to continue indefinitely? You're driven to rebellion when you think of there being no point in it and to despair when you think of there being no limit to it. That's why I find a comfort, when I feel desperate, or rebellious, or both, to remind myself of God's promise that one day it will be finished."[86]

## The Christian Call to Love

At the present we are living "in between times," between the grace which we grasp by faith and the glory which we anticipate in hope. Between them lies love.

Yet love is just what the church has generally failed to show to homosexual people. Jim Cotter complains bitterly about being treated as "objects of scorn and insult, of fear, prejudice and oppression."[87] Pittenger describes the "vituperative" correspondence he has received, in which homosexuals are dismissed even by professing Christians as "filthy creatures," "disgusting perverts," "damnable sinners," and the like.[88] Pierre Berton, a social commentator, writes that "a very good case can be made out that the homosexual is the modern equivalent of the leper."[89] Rictor Norton is yet more shrill: "The church's record regarding homosexuals is an atrocity from beginning to end: it is not for us to seek forgiveness, but for the church to make atonement."[90]

The attitude of personal antipathy towards homosexuals is nowadays termed "homophobia."[91] It is a mixture of irrational fear, hostility, and even revulsion. It overlooks the fact that the majority of homosexual people are probably not responsible for their condition (though they are, of course, for their conduct). Since they are not deliberate perverts, they deserve our understanding and compassion (though many find this patronizing), not our rejection. No wonder Richard Lovelace calls for "a double repentance," namely "that gay Christians renounce the active lifestyle" and that "straight Christians

Faith, Hope, and Love

renounce homophobia."[92] Dr. David Atkinson is right to add, "We are not at liberty to urge the Christian homosexual to celibacy and to a spreading of his relationships, unless support for the former and opportunities for the latter are available in genuine love."[93] I rather think that the very existence of the Lesbian and Gay Christian Movement is a vote of censure on the church.

At the heart of the homosexual condition is a deep loneliness, the natural human hunger for mutual love, a search for identity, and a longing for completeness. If homosexual people cannot find these things in the local "church family," we have no business to go on using that expression. The alternative is not only between the warm physical relationship of homosexual intercourse and the pain of isolation in the cold. There is a third option, namely a Christian environment of love, understanding, acceptance, and support. I do not think there is any need to encourage homosexual people to disclose their sexual inclinations to everybody; this is neither necessary nor helpful. But they do need at least one confidante to whom they can unburden themselves, who will not despise or reject them but will support them with friendship and prayer; probably some professional, private, and confidential pastoral counsel; possibly, in addition, the support of a professionally supervised therapy group; and (like all single people) many warm and affectionate friendships with people of both sexes. Same-sex friendships, like those in the Bible between Ruth and Naomi, David and Jonathan, and Paul and Timothy, are to be encouraged. There is no hint that any of these was homosexual in an erotic sense, yet they were evidently affectionate and (at least in the case of David and Jonathan) even demonstrative.[94] Of course, sensible safeguards will be important. But in African and Asian cultures it is common to see two men walking down the street hand in hand, without embarrassment. It is sad that our western culture inhibits the development of rich same-sex friendships by engendering the fear of being ridiculed or rejected as a "queer."

The best contribution of Michael Vasey's book *Strangers and Friends,* in my view, is his emphasis on friendship. "Friendship is not a minor theme of the Christian faith," he writes, "but is integral to its vision of life."[95] He sees society as "a network of friendships held together by bonds of affection." He also points out that Scripture does "not limit the notion of covenant to the institution of marriage."[96] As David and Jonathan made a covenant with each other (1 Sam. 18:3), we too may have special covenanted friendships.

These and other relationships, both same sex and opposite sex, ought to be developed within

82

the family of God, which, though universal, has its local manifestations. God intends each local church to be a warm, accepting, and supportive community. By "accepting" I do not mean "acquiescing"; similarly, by a rejection of "homophobia" I do not mean a rejection of a proper Christian disapproval of homosexual behavior. No, true love is not incompatible with the maintenance of moral standards. On the contrary, it insists on them, for the good of everybody. There is, therefore, a place for church discipline in the case of members who refuse to repent and willfully persist in homosexual relationships. But it must be exercised in a spirit of humility and gentleness (Gal. 6:1f); we must be careful not to discriminate between men and women, or between homosexual and heterosexual offenses; and necessary discipline in the case of a public scandal is not to be confused with a witch hunt.

Perplexing and painful as the homosexual Christian's dilemma is, Jesus Christ offers him or her (indeed, all of us) faith, hope, and love—the faith to accept both his standards and his grace to maintain them, the hope to look beyond present suffering to future glory, and the love to care for and support one another. "But the greatest of these is love" (1 Cor. 13:13).

# NOTES

1. See A. C. Kinsey's *Sexual Behavior in the Human Male* (1948) and *Sexual Behavior in the Human Female* (1953).

2. Merville Vincent, "God, Sex and You," *Eternity*, August 1972.

3. J. N. D. Anderson, *Morality, Law and Grace* (Tyndale, 1972), 73.

4. Malcolm Macourt, ed., *Towards a Theology of Gay Liberation* (SCM Press, 1977), 3. The quotation comes from Macourt's own introduction to the book.

5. John S. Spong, *Living in Sin? A Bishop Rethinks Human Sexuality* (Harper and Row, 1988).

6. Derrick Sherwin Bailey, *Homosexuality and the Western Christian Tradition* (Longmans, Green, 1955), 4.

7. Isa. 1:10ff; Jer. 23:14; Ezek. 16:49ff; cf. the references to pride in Ecclesiasticus 16:8 and to inhospitableness in Wisdom 19:8.

8. Matt. 10:15; 11:24; Luke 10:12.

9. Bailey gives references in the *Book of Jubilees* and the *Testaments of the Twelve Patriarchs* (op. cit., 11–20). There is an even fuller evaluation of the writings of the intertestamental period in Peter Coleman's *Christian Attitudes to Homosexuality* (SPCK, 1980), 58–85.

10. Bailey, *Homosexuality*, 27.

11. See James D. Martin in *Towards a Theology of Gay Liberation*, ed. Malcolm Macourt (SCM, 1977), 53.

12. Bailey, *Homosexuality*, 30.

13. Coleman, *Christian Attitudes*, 49.

14. See, for example, 1 Kings 14:22ff; 15:12; 22:46; and 2 Kings 23:7.

15. Bailey, *Homosexuality*, 39.

16. Coleman, *Christian Attitudes*, 95–6.

17. Ibid., 277.

18. Ibid., 101.

19. Rictor Norton in Macourt, *Towards a Theology*, 58.

20. Letha Scanzoni and Virginia R. Mollenkott, *Is the Homosexual My Neighbor?* (Harper and Row, and SCM, 1978), 111.

21. Bailey, *Homosexuality*, 1.

22. Michael Vasey, *Strangers and Friends* (Hodder and Stoughton, 1995), 46, 82–3.

23. See John Boswell, *Christianity, Social Tolerance and Homosexuality* (Chicago University Press, 1980)

and John Boswell, *Same-Sex Unions in Pre-Modern Europe* (Villard Books, 1994).

24. Richard John Neuhaus, "The Case against John Boswell," excerpted in Julie Belding and Bruce Nicholls, eds., *A Reason for Hope, Christian Perspectives on Homosexuality and Healing* (Auckland, New Zealand: The Human Relationships Foundation, 1996), 14.

25. Everett Ferguson, ed., *The Encyclopedia of Early Christianity* (Garland, 1990).

26. Vasey, *Strangers and Friends*, 116.

27. Ibid., 176–77.

28. Ibid., 117.

29. Ibid., 33.

30. Ibid., 34.

31. Norman Pittenger, *Time for Consent*, 3d ed. (SCM, 1976), 7, 73.

32. Thomas E. Schmidt, *Straight and Narrow? Compassion and Clarity in the Homosexuality Debate* (IVP, 1995), 134–35.

33. Pittenger, *Time for Consent*, 7.

34. So Coleman, *Christian Attitudes*, 50.

35. Chapter 3.3–5, quoted by Coleman, *Christian Attitudes*, 71.

36. Boswell, *Christianity, Social Tolerance and Homosexuality*, 107ff.

37. Richard B. Hays, "A Response to John Boswell's Exegesis of Romans 1," *Journal of Religious*

*Ethics* (spring 1986), 192. See also his *The Moral Vision of the New Testament* (T. and T. Clark, 1996), 383–89.

38. C. K. Barrett, *Commentary on the Epistle to the Romans* (A. and C. Black, 1962), 39.

39. C. E. B. Cranfield, Commentary on Romans in the *International Critical Commentary*, vol. 1 (T. and T. Clark, 1975), 126. He attributes the same meaning to *physis* in his comment on 1 Cor. 11:14. What the NIV translates "the very nature of things" Professor Cranfield renders "the very way God has made us."

40. *Christianity Today* (11 November 1996).

41. The Friends' report *Towards a Quaker View of Sex* (1963), 21.

42. Ibid., 36.

43. Methodist Church's Division of Social Responsibility, *A Christian Understanding of Human Sexuality* (1979), chap. 9.

44. Ibid., chap. 5.

45. Pittenger, *Time for Consent,* 31–3.

46. Jeffrey Satinover, *Homosexuality and the Politics of Truth* (Baker, 1996), 55. He is quoting from D. McWhirter and A. Mattison, *The Male Couple: How Relationships Develop* (Prentice-Hall, 1984).

47. Schmidt, *Straight and Narrow?* 108.

48. Satinover, *Homosexuality,* 51. See the whole of his chap. 3.

49. Schmidt, *Straight and Narrow?* 122. See the whole of his chap. 6.

50. *The Homosexual Movement: A Response by the Ramsey Colloquium,* first published in *First Things,* March 1994.

51. Macourt, *Towards a Theology,* 25.

52. Pittenger, *Time for Consent,* 2.

53. Ibid., 94.

54. Patrick Dixon, *The Truth about AIDS* (Kingsway, 1987), 78.

55. Quoted in Satinover, *Homosexuality,* 17. See also p. 57.

56. Statistics on AIDS taken from the UNAIDS web site (www.unaids.org). This is a good source for up-to-date information on AIDS around the world.

57. Dixon, *The Truth about AIDS,* 113. See also p. 88 and the chapter "Condoms Are Unsafe," 110–22.

58. *The Many Faces of AIDS: A Gospel Response* (United States Catholic Conference, 1987), 18.

59. Roy McCloughry and Carol Bebawi, *AIDS: A Christian Response* (Grove Ethical Studies, no. 64, 1987), 4, 18. See the theological discussion "Is AIDS the Judgment of God?" 12–19.

60. *The Many Faces of AIDS,* 6.

61. Quoted in *Christianity Today* (7 August 1987), 17.

62. The Terrence Higgins Trust, BM/AIDS, London WC1N 3XX.

63. For example, The London Lighthouse (a twenty-six-bed AIDS hospice), 178 Lancaster Road, London W11 1QU, and the internationally known

Notes

thirty-two-suite AIDS ward at the Mildmay Mission Hospital, Hackney Road, London E2 7NA. Both hospices also arrange home care. ACACIA (AIDS Care, Compassion in Action) cares for about seventy-five people with HIV/AIDS in their own homes in Manchester.

64. These were never published.

65. So Gavin Reid rightly argues in his *Beyond AIDS: The Real Crisis and the Only Hope* (Kingsway, 1987).

66. For example, Christian Action on AIDS was established in 1986 (P.O. Box 76, Hereford, HR1 1JX). Also, ACET (AIDS Care Education and Training), with an aim of developing a nationwide network of hospices, home care volunteers, and church support groups. Its address is P.O. Box 3693, London SW15 2BQ.

67. *AIDS*, a report by the Church of England's Board for Social Responsibility (GS 795, 1987), 29.

68. Alex Davidson, *The Returns of Love* (IVP, 1970), 12, 16, 49.

69. Pittenger in *Towards a Theology*, 87.

70. "The St. Andrew's Day Statement" (published on November 30, 1995) begins with three theological "Principles" relating to the Incarnate Lord (in whom we come to know both God and ourselves), the Holy Spirit (who enables us to interpret the times), and God the Father (who restores the broken creation in Christ). The statement's second half consists of three "Applications" relating to such questions as our human identity, empirical observations,

90

the reaffirmation of the good news of salvation, and the hope of final fulfillment in Christ.

Two years later *The Way Forward?* was published, with the subtitle *Christian Voices on Homosexuality and the Church*. This symposium, edited by Tim Bradshaw, consists of thirteen responses to "The St. Andrew's Day Statement" from a wide range of different viewpoints. One appreciates the call to patient and serious theological reflection. But it is inaccurate to write of "dialogue" and "diatribe" as if they were the only options. Some of us have been listening and reflecting for thirty or forty years! How long must the process continue before we are allowed to reach a conclusion? In spite of claims to the contrary, no fresh evidence has been produced which could overthrow the clear witness of Scripture and the longstanding tradition of the church.

"The St. Andrew's Day Statement" says that the church recognizes two vocations (marriage and singleness) and adds that "there is no place for the church to confer legitimacy upon alternatives to these." Further, the authors of the statement do not consider that "the considerable burden of proof to support a major change in the Church's teaching and practice has been met" by the contributors to the book (p. 3). Yet the book makes a more uncertain sound than the statement. So by all means let there be serious theological reflection, but then let the church make up its mind.

Notes                                                    91

71. Pittenger, *Time for Consent*, 7. Cf. *The Courage to Be Chaste*, "an uncompromising call to the biblical standard of chastity" (Paulist Press, 1986). Written by Benedict J. Groeschel, a Capuchin friar, the book contains much practical advice.

72. Satinover, *Homosexuality*, 117.

73. Ibid., 18–19, 71.

74. Vasey, *Strangers and Friends*, 103.

75. See Satinover, *Homosexuality*, 31–40.

76. D. J. West, *Homosexuality* (1955; 2d ed., Pelican, 1960; 3d ed., Duckworth, 1968), 266, 273.

77. Nelson González's article "Exploding Ex-Gay Myths" (*Regeneration Quarterly* 1, no. 3, summer 1995) challenged the aims and claims of the ex-gay movement. In 1991 Charles Socarides founded the National Association for Research and Therapy of Homosexuality (NARTH), which investigates the possibilities for "healing."

78. Martin Hallett, *I Am Learning to Love* (Marshall, Morgan, and Scott, 1987), 155. Martin Hallett's organization is called True Freedom Trust (P.O. Box 3, Upton, Wirral, Merseyside, L49 6NY). It offers an interdenominational teaching and counseling ministry on homosexuality and related problems.

79. P.O. Box 2121, San Rafael, CA 94912.

80. *Christianity Today* (18 August 1989).

81. Elizabeth R. Moberly, *Homosexuality: A New Christian Ethic* (James Clarke, 1983), 2. See also *No-Gay Areas: Pastoral Care of Homosexual Christians*

(Grove Pastoral Studies no. 38, 1989) by Lance Pierson, who helpfully applies Dr. Moberly's teaching.

82. Ibid., 28.

83. Ibid., 18–20.

84. Ibid., 35–36.

85. Ibid., 52.

86. Davidson, *The Returns of Love*, 51.

87. Macourt, *Towards a Theology*, 63.

88. Pittenger, *Time for Consent*, 2.

89. Quoted from Letha Scanzoni and Virginia Mollenkott, *The Comfortable Pew* (1965).

90. Macourt, *Towards a Theology*, 45.

91. The word seems to have been used first by George Weinberg in *Society and the Healthy Homosexual* (Doubleday, 1973).

92. Richard R. Lovelace, *Homosexuality and the Church* (Revell, 1978), 129, cf. 125.

93. David J. Atkinson, *Homosexuals in the Christian Fellowship* (Latimer House, 1979), 118. See also Dr. Atkinson's more extensive treatment in his *Pastoral Ethics in Practice* (Monarch, 1989). Dr. Roger Moss concentrates on pastoral questions in his *Christians and Homosexuality* (Paternoster, 1977).

94. E.g., 1 Sam. 18:1–4; 20:41; and 2 Sam. 1:26.

95. Vasey, *Strangers and Friends*, 122.

96. Ibid., 233.

John Stott is rector emeritus of All Souls Church, London, England. He is widely respected as a New Testament scholar, author, and leader in the Church's worldwide mission, and is the president of the London Institute for Contemporary Christianity. His books include *Basic Christianity* and *Christian Counter-Culture*.